Plants

Seeds

Patricia Whitehouse

www.raintreepublishers.co.uk

Visit our website to find out more information about **Raintree** books.

To order:

 Phone 44 (0) 1865 888112

Send a fax to 44 (0) 1865 314091

Visit the Raintree Bookshop at **www.raintreepublishers.co.uk** to browse our catalogue and order online.

First published in Great Britain by Raintree, Halley Court, Jordan Hill, Oxford OX2 8EJ, part of Harcourt Education.
Raintree is a registered trademark of Harcourt Education Ltd.

© Harcourt Education Ltd 2003
First published in paperback in 2004
The moral right of the proprietor has been asserted.

Editorial: Nick Hunter and Diyan Leake
Design: Sue Emerson (HL-US) and Joanna Sapwell (www.tipani.co.uk)
Picture Research: Amor Montes de Oca (HL-US)
Production: Jonathan Smith

Originated by Dot Gradations
Printed and bound in China by South China Printing Company

10 digit ISBN 1 844 21067 7 (hardback)
13 digit ISBN 978 1 844 21067 1 (hardback)
07 06 05 04 03
10 9 8 7 6 5 4 3 2 1
10 digit ISBN 1 844 21074 X (paperback)
13 digit ISBN 978 1 844 21074 9 (paperback)
07 06
10 9 8 7 6 5 4 3 2

British Library Cataloguing in Publication Data
Whitehouse, Patricia
Seeds
575.6'8
A full catalogue record for this book is available from the British Library.

Acknowledgements
The publishers would like to thank the following for permission to reproduce photographs: Amor Montes de Oca p. **5R**; Bruce Coleman Inc. pp. **5L** (Michael Gadomski), **12** (Danny Camilli), **23** (pine cones, Michael Gadomski; point, E. R. Degginger; stone, Danny Camilli); Color Pic, Inc. pp. **1** (E. R. Degginger), **14** (E. R. Degginger), **16** (E. R. Degginger), **22** (seeds, E. R. Degginger), **24** (seeds, E. R. Degginger); Corbis pp. **17** (Frank Lane Picture Agency), **19** (Lynda Richardson), back cover (sunflower seeds, Frank Lane Picture Agency); Craig Mitchelldyer p. **13**; David June pp. **11**, **23** (stone); Dwight Kuhn pp. **7**, **15L**, **21**, **22** (wings), **23** (wings), **24** (wings); Rick Wetherbee p. **18**; Rob and Ann Simpson p. **20**; Visuals Unlimited pp. **4** (Images International), **6** (Jerome Wexler), **8** (Mary Cummings), **9** (Tom Edwards), **10** (Wally Eberhart), **15** (hooks, Walt Anderson), **22** (hooks, Walt Anderson), **23** (fruit, Tome Edwards; hooks, Walt Anderson; seedling, Jerome Wexler), **24** (hooks, Walt Anderson), back cover (fruit, Images International).

Cover photograph of sunflower seeds reproduced with permission of Corbis (Frank Lane Picture Agency)

Every effort has been made to contact copyright holders of any material reproduced in this book. Any omissions will be rectified in subsequent printings if notice is given to the publishers.

Some words are shown in bold, **like this.** You can find them in the glossary on page 23.

Contents

What are seeds? 4

Why do plants have seeds? 6

Where are the seeds on a plant? 8

How big are seeds? 10

How many seeds can a plant have? . . . 12

Why do seeds have different shapes? . . . 14

What colours are seeds? 16

How do people use seeds? 18

How do animals use seeds? 20

Quiz 22

Glossary 23

Index 24

Answers to quiz 24

What are seeds?

Seeds are part of a plant.

Some seeds are inside **fruits** and vegetables.

pine cones

pine seeds

Some seeds are inside **pine cones**.

The seeds come out when the pine cone opens up.

Why do plants have seeds?

Seeds make new plants.

The new plants are called **seedlings**.

The new plants look just like the plant the seeds came from.

Where are the seeds on a plant?

The flowers of a plant make seeds.

The seeds are part of the **fruit** of a plant.

The seeds might be on the fruit.

They might be inside it.

How big are seeds?

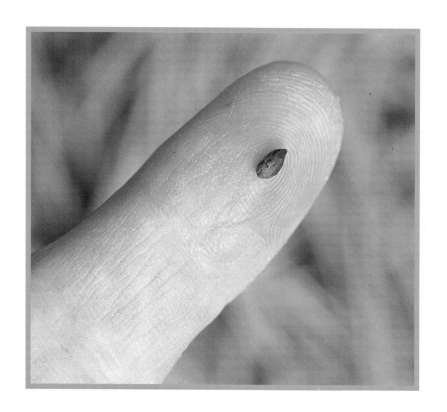

Seeds come in many sizes.

Some seeds are tiny.

Some seeds are very big.

A coconut is a very big seed.

How many seeds can a plant have?

A **fruit** may have just one seed.

An avocado seed is called a **stone**.

Some plants have hundreds of seeds.

Dandelion seeds fly away when you blow on them.

Why do seeds have different shapes?

seed points

The shape of a seed helps it move to a place where it will grow.

Some seeds have points that push into the soil.

seed wings

seed hooks

Wings help some seeds blow in the wind.

Hooks help other seeds hold on to things.

What colours are seeds?

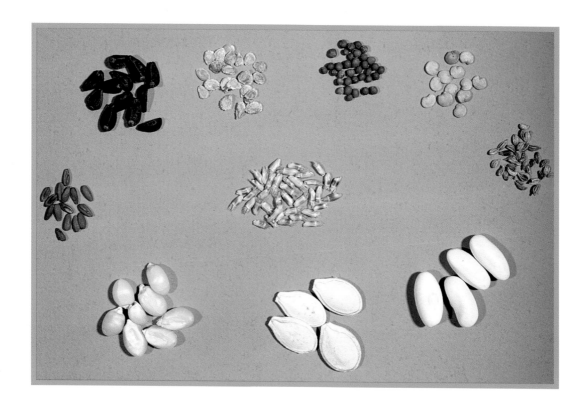

Seeds can be black, brown or yellow.

They can be other colours, too.

Some seeds have patterns on them.

These sunflower seeds have stripes.

How do people use seeds?

People use seeds for food.

We eat some seeds just the way they are.

We crush, squeeze or pop some seeds before we eat them.

We can put seeds in the ground to grow new plants.

How do animals use seeds?

Animals use seeds for food, too.

Birds, squirrels, elephants and monkeys eat seeds.

Some animals eat the seeds
right away.

Others save their seeds to
eat later.

Quiz

Can you remember what these seeds do?

Look for the answers on page 24.

?

?

?

Glossary

fruit
part of a plant where the seeds are

hook
curved part that catches on to things

pine cone
fruit of the pine tree

point
sharp end

seedling
new plant that has just come out of the ground

stone
the name for a seed if there is only one in a fruit

wing
part that helps seeds move through the air

Index

animals   20, 21

colours   16

flowers   8

food   18, 20

fruits   4, 8, 9, 12, 23

hooks   15, 23

patterns   17

people   18, 19

pine cones   5, 23

points   14, 23

seedlings   6, 23

shapes   14

sizes   10

soil   14

stones   12, 23

vegetables   4

wings   15, 23

Answers to quiz on
page 22

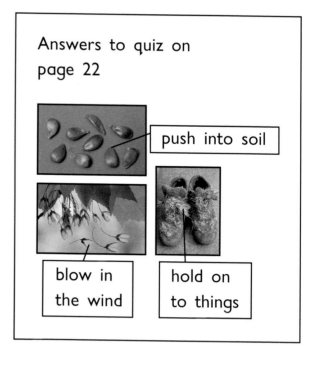

push into soil

blow in
the wind

hold on
to things